# FAVORITE POEMS of the WILD

## AN ADVENTURER'S COLLECTION

Published by Bushel & Peck Books, a family-run publishing house in Fresno, California,
that believes in uplifting children with the highest standards of art, music, literature, and
ideas. Find beautiful books for gifted young minds at www.bushelandpeckbooks.com.

Type set in Temeraire and Baskerville.
Mountain engraving by Very_Very/Shutterstock.com
Leaf engraving by MoreVector/Shutterstock.com

Designed by David Miles.

Bushel & Peck Books is dedicated to fighting illiteracy all over the world. For every
book we sell, we donate one to a child in need—book for book. To nominate a school or
organization to receive free books, please visit www.bushelandpeckbooks.com.

ISBN: 9781638191049

First Edition

Printed in the United States

10 9 8 7 6 5 4 3 2 1

# FAVORITE
# POEMS
## *of the* WILD

AN ADVENTURER'S
COLLECTION

BUSHEL
& PECK
BOOKS

# CONTENTS

# IN THE MOUNTAINS ON A SUMMER DAY

*Li Po*

Gently I stir a white feather fan,
With open shirt, sitting in a green wood.
I take off my cap and hang it on a jutting stone:
A wind from the pine-trees trickles on my bare head.

# NATURE

*Henry David Thoreau*

O Nature! I do not aspire
To be the highest in thy quire,—
To be a meteor in the sky,
Or comet that may range on high;
Only a zephyr that may blow
Among the reeds by the river low;
Give me thy most privy place
Where to run my airy race.
In some withdrawn, unpublic mead
Let me sigh upon a reed,
Or in the woods, with leafy din,
Whisper the still evening in
Some still work give me to do,—
Only—be it near to you!
For I'd rather be thy child
And pupil, in the forest wild,
Than be the king of men elsewhere,

And most sovereign slave of care:
To have one moment of thy dawn,
Than share the city's year forlorn.

# SUMMER STORM

*James Russell Lowell*

Untremulous in the river clear,
Toward the sky's image, hangs the imaged bridge
So still the air that I can hear
The slender clarion of the unseen midge;
Out of the stillness, with a gathering creep,
Like rising wind in leaves, which now decreases,
Now lulls, now swells, and all the while increases,
    The huddling trample of a drove of sheep
Tilts the loose planks, and then as gradually ceases
    In dust on the other side; life's emblem deep,
A confused noise between two silences,
Finding at last in dust precarious peace.
On the wide marsh the purple-blossomed grasses
    Soak up the sunshine; sleeps the brimming tide
Save when the wedge-shaped wake in silence passes
    Of some slow water-rat, whose sinuous glide
    Wavers the long green sedge's shade from side to side;
But up the west, like a rock-shivered surge,

Climbs a great cloud edged with sun-whitened spray;
Huge whirls of foam boil toppling o'er its verge,
  And falling still it seems, and yet it climbs alway.


    Suddenly all the sky is hid
    As with the shutting of a lid,
One by one great drops are falling
    Doubtful and slow,
Down the pane they are crookedly crawling,
    And the wind breathes low;
Slowly the circles widen on the river,
    Widen and mingle, one and all;
Here and there the slenderer flowers shiver,
    Struck by an icy rain-drop's fall.


Now on the hills I hear the thunder mutter,
    The wind is gathering in the west;
The upturned leaves first whiten and flutter,
    Then droop to a fitful rest;
Up from the stream with sluggish flap
    Struggles the gull and floats away;
Nearer and nearer rolls the thunder-clap,—
    We shall not see the sun go down to-day:

Now leaps the wind on the sleepy marsh,
  And tramples the grass with terrified feet,
The startled river turns leaden and harsh.
  You can hear the quick heart of the tempest beat.

    Look! look! that livid flash!
And instantly follows the rattling thunder,
As if some cloud-crag, split asunder,
      Fell, splintering with a ruinous crash,
On the Earth, which crouches in silence under;
  And now a solid gray wall of rain
Shuts off the landscape, mile by mile;
  For a breath's space I see the blue wood again,
And, ere the next heart-beat, the wind-hurled pile,
    That seemed but now a league aloof,
    Bursts crackling o'er the sun-parched roof;
Against the windows the storm comes dashing,
Through tattered foliage the hail tears crashing,
      The blue lightning flashes,
      The rapid hail clashes,
    The white waves are tumbling,
      And, in one baffled roar,
    Like the toothless sea mumbling

A rock-bristled shore,
The thunder is rumbling
And crashing and crumbling,—
Will silence return never more?

Hush! Still as death,
The tempest holds his breath
As from a sudden will;
The rain stops short, but from the eaves
You see it drop, and hear it from the leaves,
All is so bodingly still;
Again, now, now, again
Plashes the rain in heavy gouts,
The crinkled lightning
Seems ever brightening,
And loud and long
Again the thunder shouts
His battle-song,—
One quivering flash,
One wildering crash,
Followed by silence dead and dull,
As if the cloud, let go,
Leapt bodily below

To whelm the earth in one mad overthrow,
    And then a total lull.

      Gone, gone, so soon!
  No more my half-crazed fancy there
  Can shape a giant in the air,
  No more I see his streaming hair,
  The writhing portent of his form;—
    The pale and quiet moon
  Makes her calm forehead bare,
  And the last fragments of the storm,
Like shattered rigging from a fight at sea,
Silent and few, are drifting over me.

# THE MOUNTAIN

*Emily Dickinson*

The mountain sat upon the plain
In his eternal chair,
His observation omnifold,
His inquest everywhere.

The seasons prayed around his knees,
Like children round a sire:
Grandfather of the days is he,
Of dawn the ancestor.

# LEAVES

*Sara Teasdale*

ONE by one, like leaves from a tree,
All my faiths have forsaken me;
But the stars above my head
Burn in white and delicate red,
And beneath my feet the earth
Brings the sturdy grass to birth.
I who was content to be
But a silken-singing tree,
But a rustle of delight
In the wistful heart of night—
I have lost the leaves that knew
Touch of rain and weight of dew.
Blinded by a leafy crown
I looked neither up nor down—
But the little leaves that die
Have left me room to see the sky;
Now for the first time I know
Stars above and earth below.

# THE HEAVENS

*Ralph Waldo Emerson*

Wisp and meteor nightly falling,
But the Stars of God remain.

# NIGHT IN A CANOE

*Samuel Hall Young*

A dreary world! The constant rain
      Beats back to earth blithe fancy's wings;
      And life—a sodden garment—clings
About a body numb with pain.

Imagination ceased with light;
      Of Nature's psalm no echo lingers.
      The death-cold mist, with ghostly fingers,
Shrouds world and soul in rayless night.

An inky sea, a sullen crew,
      A frail canoe's uncertain motion;
      A whispered talk of wind and ocean,
As plotting secret crimes to do!

The vampire-night sucks all my blood;
      Warm home and love seem lost for aye;

From cloud to cloud I steal away,
Like guilty soul o'er Stygian flood.

Peace, morbid heart! From paddle blade
    See the black water flash in light;
    And bars of moonbeams streaming white,
Have pearls of ebon raindrops made.

From darkest sea of deep despair
    Gleams Hope, awaked by Action's blow;
    And Faith's clear ray, though clouds hang low,
Slants up to heights serene and fair.

# HYMN BEFORE SUN-RISE, IN THE VALE OF CHAMOUNI

*Samuel Taylor Coleridge*

Hast thou a charm to stay the morning-star
In his steep course? So long he seems to pause
On thy bald awful head, O sovran Blanc,
The Arve and Arveiron at thy base
Rave ceaselessly; but thou, most awful Form!
Risest from forth thy silent sea of pines,
How silently! Around thee and above
Deep is the air and dark, substantial, black,
An ebon mass: methinks thou piercest it,
As with a wedge! But when I look again,
It is thine own calm home, thy crystal shrine,
Thy habitation from eternity!
O dread and silent Mount! I gazed upon thee,
Till thou, still present to the bodily sense,
Didst vanish from my thought: entranced in prayer
I worshipped the Invisible alone.
Yet, like some sweet beguiling melody,

So sweet, we know not we are listening to it,

Thou, the meanwhile, wast blending with my Thought,

Yea, with my Life and Life's own secret joy:

Till the dilating Soul, enrapt, transfused,

Into the mighty vision passing—there

As in her natural form, swelled vast to Heaven!

Awake, my soul! not only passive praise

Thou owest! not alone these swelling tears,

Mute thanks and secret ecstasy! Awake,

Voice of sweet song! Awake, my heart, awake!

Green vales and icy cliffs, all join my Hymn.

Thou first and chief, sole sovereign of the Vale!

O struggling with the darkness all the night,

And visited all night by troops of stars,

Or when they climb the sky or when they sink:

Companion of the morning-star at dawn,

Thyself Earth's rosy star, and of the dawn

Co-herald: wake, O wake, and utter praise!

Who sank thy sunless pillars deep in Earth?

Who filled thy countenance with rosy light?

Who made thee parent of perpetual streams?

And you, ye five wild torrents fiercely glad!

Who called you forth from night and utter death,

From dark and icy caverns called you forth,

Down those precipitous, black, jagged rocks,

For ever shattered and the same for ever?

Who gave you your invulnerable life,

Your strength, your speed, your fury, and your joy,

Unceasing thunder and eternal foam?

And who commanded (and the silence came),

Here let the billows stiffen, and have rest?

Ye Ice-falls! ye that from the mountain's brow

Adown enormous ravines slope amain—

Torrents, methinks, that heard a mighty voice,

And stopped at once amid their maddest plunge!

Motionless torrents! silent cataracts!

Who made you glorious as the Gates of Heaven

Beneath the keen full moon? Who bade the sun

Clothe you with rainbows? Who, with living flowers

Of loveliest blue, spread garlands at your feet?—

God! let the torrents, like a shout of nations,

Answer! and let the ice-plains echo, God!

God! sing ye meadow-streams with gladsome voice!

Ye pine-groves, with your soft and soul-like sounds!

And they too have a voice, yon piles of snow,

And in their perilous fall shall thunder, God!

Ye living flowers that skirt the eternal frost!

Ye wild goats sporting round the eagle's nest!

Ye eagles, play-mates of the mountain-storm!

Ye lightnings, the dread arrows of the clouds!
Ye signs and wonders of the element!
Utter forth God, and fill the hills with praise!
Thou too, hoar Mount! with thy sky-pointing peaks,
Oft from whose feet the avalanche, unheard,
Shoots downward, glittering through the pure serene
Into the depth of clouds, that veil thy breast—
Thou too again, stupendous Mountain! thou
That as I raise my head, awhile bowed low
In adoration, upward from thy base
Slow travelling with dim eyes suffused with tears,
Solemnly seemest, like a vapoury cloud,
To rise before me—Rise, O ever rise,
Rise like a cloud of incense from the Earth!
Thou kingly Spirit throned among the hills,
Thou dread ambassador from Earth to Heaven,
Great Hierarch! tell thou the silent sky,
And tell the stars, and tell yon rising sun
Earth, with her thousand voices, praises God.

# LOUD WITHOUT THE WIND
# WAS ROARING

*Emily Brontë*

Loud without the wind was roaring
Through th'autumnal sky;
Drenching wet, the cold rain pouring,
Spoke of winter nigh.
All too like that dreary eve,
Did my exiled spirit grieve.
Grieved at first, but grieved not long,
Sweet—how softly sweet!—it came;
Wild words of an ancient song,
Undefined, without a name.

"It was spring, and the skylark was singing:"
Those words they awakened a spell;
They unlocked a deep fountain, whose springing,
Nor absence, nor distance can quell.

In the gloom of a cloudy November

They uttered the music of May;
They kindled the perishing ember
Into fervour that could not decay.

Awaken, o'er all my dear moorland,
West-wind, in thy glory and pride!
Oh! call me from valley and lowland,
To walk by the hill-torrent's side!

It is swelled with the first snowy weather;
The rocks they are icy and hoar,
And sullenly waves the long heather,
And the fern leaves are sunny no more.

There are no yellow stars on the mountain
The bluebells have long died away
From the brink of the moss-bedded fountain—
From the side of the wintry brae.

But lovelier than corn-fields all waving
In emerald, and vermeil, and gold,
Are the heights where the north-wind is raving,
And the crags where I wandered of old.

It was morning: the bright sun was beaming;
How sweetly it brought back to me

The time when nor labour nor dreaming
Broke the sleep of the happy and free!

But blithely we rose as the dawn-heaven
Was melting to amber and blue,
And swift were the wings to our feet given,
As we traversed the meadows of dew.

For the moors! For the moors, where the short grass
Like velvet beneath us should lie!
For the moors! For the moors, where each high pass
Rose sunny against the clear sky!

For the moors, where the linnet was trilling
Its song on the old granite stone;
Where the lark, the wild sky-lark, was filling
Every breast with delight like its own!

What language can utter the feeling
Which rose, when in exile afar,
On the brow of a lonely hill kneeling,
I saw the brown heath growing there?

It was scattered and stunted, and told me
That soon even that would be gone:
It whispered, "The grim walls enfold me,
I have bloomed in my last summer's sun."

But not the loved music, whose waking
Makes the soul of the Swiss die away,
Has a spell more adored and heartbreaking
Than, for me, in that blighted heath lay.

The spirit which bent 'neath its power,
How it longed—how it burned to be free!
If I could have wept in that hour,
Those tears had been heaven to me.

Well—well; the sad minutes are moving,
Though loaded with trouble and pain;
And some time the loved and the loving
Shall meet on the mountains again!

# THE FALLEN TREE

*Alfred Castner King*

I passed along a mountain road,
    Which led me through a wooded glen,
Remote from dwelling or abode
    And ordinary haunts of men;
        And wearied from the dust and heat.
        Beneath a tree, I found a seat.

The tree, a tall majestic spruce,
    Which had, perhaps for centuries,
Withstood, without a moment's truce,
    The wing-ed warfare of the breeze;
        A monarch of the solitude,
        Which well might grace the noblest wood.

Beneath its cool and welcome shade,
    Protected from the noontide rays,
The birds amid its branches played
    And caroled forth their twittering praise;

A squirrel perched upon a limb
And chattered with loquacious vim.

E'er yet that selfsame week had sped,
On my return, I sought its shade;
But where it reared its form, instead;
A fallen monarch I surveyed,
Prostrate and broken on the ground,
Nor longer cast its shade around.

Uprooted and disheveled, there
The monarch of the forest lay;
As if in desolate despair
Its last resistance fell away,
And overwhelmed, in evil hour
Went down before the tempest's power.

Such are the final works of fate;
The birds to other branches flew;
And man, whatever his estate,
Must face that same mutation, too!
To-day, I stand erect and tall,
The morrow—may record my fall.

# MONT BLANC

*Percy Bysshe Shelley*

## 1.

The everlasting universe of things
Flows through the mind, and rolls its rapid waves,
Now dark—now glittering—now reflecting gloom—
Now lending splendour, where from secret springs
The source of human thought its tribute brings
Of waters,—with a sound but half its own,
Such as a feeble brook will oft assume
In the wild woods, among the mountains lone,
Where waterfalls around it leap for ever,
Where woods and winds contend, and a vast river
Over its rocks ceaselessly bursts and raves.

## 2.

Thus thou, Ravine of Arve—dark, deep Ravine—

Thou many-coloured, many-voiced vale,
Over whose pines, and crags, and caverns sail
Fast cloud-shadows and sunbeams: awful scene,
Where Power in likeness of the Arve comes down
From the ice-gulfs that gird his secret throne,
Bursting through these dark mountains like the flame
Of lightning through the tempest;—thou dost lie,
Thy giant brood of pines around thee clinging,
Children of elder time, in whose devotion
The chainless winds still come and ever came
To drink their odours, and their mighty swinging
To hear—an old and solemn harmony;
Thine earthly rainbows stretched across the sweep
Of the ethereal waterfall, whose veil
Robes some unsculptured image; the strange sleep
Which when the voices of the desert fail
Wraps all in its own deep eternity;—
Thy caverns echoing to the Arve's commotion,
A loud, lone sound no other sound can tame;
Thou art pervaded with that ceaseless motion,
Thou art the path of that unresting sound—
Dizzy Ravine! and when I gaze on thee
I seem as in a trance sublime and strange
To muse on my own separate fantasy,

My own, my human mind, which passively
Now renders and receives fast influencings,
Holding an unremitting interchange
With the clear universe of things around;
One legion of wild thoughts, whose wandering wings
Now float above thy darkness, and now rest
Where that or thou art no unbidden guest,
In the still cave of the witch Poesy,
Seeking among the shadows that pass by
Ghosts of all things that are, some shade of thee,
Some phantom, some faint image; till the breast
From which they fled recalls them, thou art there!


### 3.

Some say that gleams of a remoter world
Visit the soul in sleep,—that death is slumber,
And that its shapes the busy thoughts outnumber
Of those who wake and live.—I look on high;
Has some unknown omnipotence unfurled
The veil of life and death? or do I lie
In dream, and does the mightier world of sleep
Spread far around and inaccessibly
Its circles? For the very spirit fails,
Driven like a homeless cloud from steep to steep

That vanishes among the viewless gales!
Far, far above, piercing the infinite sky,
Mont Blanc appears,—still, snowy, and serene—
Its subject mountains their unearthly forms
Pile around it, ice and rock; broad vales between
Of frozen floods, unfathomable deeps,
Blue as the overhanging heaven, that spread
And wind among the accumulated steeps;
A desert peopled by the storms alone,
Save when the eagle brings some hunter's bone,
And the wolf tracts her there—how hideously
Its shapes are heaped around! rude, bare, and high,
Ghastly, and scarred, and riven.—Is this the scene
Where the old Earthquake-daemon taught her young
Ruin? Were these their toys? or did a sea
Of fire envelope once this silent snow?
None can reply—all seems eternal now.
The wilderness has a mysterious tongue
Which teaches awful doubt, or faith so mild,
So solemn, so serene, that man may be,
But for such faith, with nature reconciled;
Thou hast a voice, great Mountain, to repeal
Large codes of fraud and woe; not understood
By all, but which the wise, and great, and good
Interpret, or make felt, or deeply feel.

## 4.

The fields, the lakes, the forests, and the streams,
Ocean, and all the living things that dwell
Within the daedal earth; lightning, and rain,
Earthquake, and fiery flood, and hurricane,
The torpor of the year when feeble dreams
Visit the hidden buds, or dreamless sleep
Holds every future leaf and flower;—the bound
With which from that detested trance they leap;
The works and ways of man, their death and birth,
And that of him and all that his may be;
All things that move and breathe with toil and sound
Are born and die; revolve, subside, and swell.
Power dwells apart in its tranquillity,
Remote, serene, and inaccessible:
And THIS, the naked countenance of earth,
On which I gaze, even these primaeval mountains
Teach the adverting mind. The glaciers creep
Like snakes that watch their prey, from their far fountains,
Slow rolling on; there, many a precipice,
Frost and the Sun in scorn of mortal power
Have piled: dome, pyramid, and pinnacle,

A city of death, distinct with many a tower
And wall impregnable of beaming ice.
Yet not a city, but a flood of ruin
Is there, that from the boundaries of the sky
Rolls its perpetual stream; vast pines are strewing
Its destined path, or in the mangled soil
Branchless and shattered stand; the rocks, drawn down
From yon remotest waste, have overthrown
The limits of the dead and living world,
Never to be reclaimed. The dwelling-place
Of insects, beasts, and birds, becomes its spoil;
Their food and their retreat for ever gone,
So much of life and joy is lost. The race
Of man flies far in dread; his work and dwelling
Vanish, like smoke before the tempest's stream,
And their place is not known. Below, vast caves
Shine in the rushing torrents' restless gleam,
Which from those secret chasms in tumult welling
Meet in the vale, and one majestic River,
The breath and blood of distant lands, for ever
Rolls its loud waters to the ocean waves,
Breathes its swift vapours to the circling air.

5.

Mont Blanc yet gleams on high—the power is there,
The still and solemn power of many sights,
And many sounds, and much of life and death.
In the calm darkness of the moonless nights,
In the lone glare of day, the snows descend
Upon that Mountain; none beholds them there,
Nor when the flakes burn in the sinking sun,
Or the star-beams dart through them:—Winds contend
Silently there, and heap the snow with breath
Rapid and strong, but silently! Its home
The voiceless lightning in these solitudes
Keeps innocently, and like vapour broods
Over the snow. The secret strength of things
Which governs thought, and to the infinite dome
Of heaven is as a law, inhabits thee!
And what were thou, and earth, and stars, and sea,
If to the human mind's imaginings
Silence and solitude were vacancy?

# CLEARING UP AT DAWN

*Li Po*

The fields are chill; the sparse rain has stopped;
The colours of Spring teem on every side.
With leaping fish the blue pond is full;
With singing thrushes the green boughs droop.
The flowers of the field have dabbled their
    powdered cheeks;
The mountain grasses are bent level at the waist.
By the bamboo stream the last fragments of cloud
Blown by the wind slowly scatter away.

# GREEN MOUNTAINS

*James Russell Lowell*

Ye mountains, that far off lift up your heads,
Seen dimly through their canopies of blue,
The shade of my unrestful spirit sheds
Distance-created beauty over you;
I am not well content with this far view;
How may I know what foot of loved-one treads
Your rocks moss-grown and sun-dried torrent beds?
We should love all things better, if we knew
What claims the meanest have upon our hearts:
Perchance even now some eye, that would be bright
To meet my own, looks on your mist-robed forms;
Perchance your grandeur a deep joy imparts
To souls that have encircled mine with light—
O brother-heart, with thee my spirit warms!

### X.

My friend, adown Life's valley, hand in hand,
With grateful change of grave and merry speech

Or song, our hearts unlocking each to each,
We'll journey onward to the silent land;
And when stern Death shall loose that loving band,
Taking in his cold hand a hand of ours,
The one shall strew the other's grave with flowers,
Nor shall his heart a moment be unmanned.
My friend and brother! if thou goest first,
Wilt thou no more re-visit me below?
Yea, when my heart seems happy, causelessly
And swells, not dreaming why, as it would burst
With joy unspeakable—my soul shall know
That thou, unseen, art bending over me.

### XI.

Verse cannot say how beautiful thou art,
How glorious the calmness of thine eyes,
Full of unconquerable energies,
Telling that thou hast acted well thy part.
No doubt or fear thy steady faith can start,
No thought of evil dare come nigh to thee,
Who hast the courage meek of purity,
The self-stayed greatness of a loving heart,
Strong with serene, enduring fortitude;
Where'er thou art, that seems thy fitting place,
For not of forms, but Nature, art thou child;
And lowest things put on a noble grace

When touched by ye, O patient, Ruth-like, mild
And spotless hands of earnest womanhood.

### XII.

The soul would fain its loving kindness tell,
But custom hangs like lead upon the tongue;
The heart is brimful, hollow crowds among,
When it finds one whose life and thought are well;
Up to the eyes its gushing love doth swell,
The angel cometh and the waters move,
Yet it is fearful still to say "I love,"
And words come grating as a jangled bell.
O might we only speak but what we feel,
Might the tongue pay but what the heart doth owe,
Not Heaven's great thunder, when, deep peal on peal,
It shakes the earth, could rouse our spirits so,
Or to the soul such majesty reveal,
As two short words half-spoken faint and low!

### XIII.

I saw a gate: a harsh voice spake and said,
"This is the gate of Life;" above was writ,
"Leave hope behind, all ye who enter it;"
Then shrank my heart within itself for dread;
But, softer than the summer rain is shed,

Words dropt upon my soul, and they did say,
"Fear nothing, Faith shall save thee, watch and pray!"
So, without fear I lifted up my head,
And lo! that writing was not, one fair word
Was carven in its stead, and it was "Love."
Then rained once more those sweet tones from above
With healing on their wings: I humbly heard,
"I am the Life, ask and it shall be given!
I am the way, by me ye enter Heaven!"

### XIV.

To the dark, narrow house where loved ones go,
Whence no steps outward turn, whose silent door
None but the sexton knocks at any more,
Are they not sometimes with us yet below?
The longings of the soul would tell us so;
Although, so pure and fine their being's essence,
Our bodily eyes are witless of their presence,
Yet not within the tomb their spirits glow,
Like wizard lamps pent up, but whensoever
With great thoughts worthy of their high behests
Our souls are filled, those bright ones with us be,
As, in the patriarch's tent, his angel guests;—
O let us live so worthily, that never
We may be far from that blest company.

## XV.

I fain would give to thee the loveliest things,
For lovely things belong to thee of right,
And thou hast been as peaceful to my sight,
As the still thoughts that summer twilight brings;
Beneath the shadow of thine angel wings
O let me live! O let me rest in thee,
Growing to thee more and more utterly,
Upbearing and upborn, till outward things
Are only as they share in thee a part!
Look kindly on me, let thy holy eyes
Bless me from the deep fulness of thy heart;
So shall my soul in its right strength arise,
And nevermore shall pine and shrink and start,
Safe-sheltered in thy full souled sympathies.

## XVI.

Much I had mused of Love, and in my soul
There was one chamber where I dared not look,
So much its dark and dreary voidness shook
My spirit, feeling that I was not whole:
All my deep longings flowed toward one goal
For long, long years, but were not answerèd,
Till Hope was drooping, Faith well-nigh stone-dead,

And I was still a blind, earth-delving mole;
Yet did I know that God was wise and good,
And would fulfil my being late or soon;
Nor was such thought in vain, for, seeing thee,
Great Love rose up, as, o'er a black pine wood,
Round, bright, and clear, upstarteth the full moon,
Filling my soul with glory utterly.

## XVII.

Sayest thou, most beautiful, that thou wilt wear
Flowers and leafy crowns when thou art old,
And that thy heart shall never grow so cold
But they shall love to wreath thy silvered hair
And into age's snows the hope of spring-tide bear?
O, in thy child-like wisdom's moveless hold
Dwell ever! still the blessings manifold
Of purity, of peace, and untaught care
For other's hearts, around thy pathway shed,
And thou shalt have a crown of deathless flowers
To glorify and guard thy blessèd head
And give their freshness to thy life's last hours;
And, when the Bridegroom calleth, they shall be
A wedding-garment white as snow for thee.

## XVIII.

Poet! who sittest in thy pleasant room,
Warming thy heart with idle thoughts of love,
And of a holy life that leads above,
Striving to keep life's spring-flowers still in bloom,
And lingering to snuff their fresh perfume—
O, there were other duties meant for thee,
Than to sit down in peacefulness and Be!
O, there are brother-hearts that dwell in gloom,
Souls loathsome, foul, and black with daily sin,
So crusted o'er with baseness, that no ray
Of heaven's blessed light may enter in!
Come down, then, to the hot and dusty way,
And lead them back to hope and peace again—
For, save in Act, thy Love is all in vain.

# TO THE PINES

*Alfred Castner King*

Ye sad musicians of the wood,

Whose dirges fill the solitude,

Whose minor strains and melodies

Are wafted on the whispering breeze,

Whose plaintive chants and listless sighs,

Ascend as incense to the skies;

Do solemn tones afford relief,

With you, as men, a vent for grief?

# THUNDER BAY

*Samuel Hall Young*

Deep calm from God enfolds the land;
Light on the mountain top I stand;
How peaceful all, but ah, how grand!

Low lies the bay beneath my feet;
The bergs sail out, a white-winged fleet,
To where the sky and ocean meet.

Their glacier mother sleeps between
Her granite walls. The mountains lean
Above her, trailing skirts of green.

Each ancient brow is raised to heaven:
The snow streams always, tempest-driven,
Like hoary locks, o'er chasms riven

By throes of Earth. But, still as sleep,
No storm disturbs the quiet deep
Where mirrored forms their silence keep.

A heaven of light beneath the sea!
A dream of worlds from shadow free!
A pictured, bright eternity!

The azure domes above, below
(A crystal casket), hold and show,
As precious jewels, gems of snow,

Dark emerald islets, amethyst
Of far horizon, pearls of mist
In pendant clouds, clear icebergs, kissed

By wavelets,—sparkling diamonds rare
Quick flashing through the ambient air.
A ring of mountains, graven fair

In lines of grace, encircles all,
Save where the purple splendors fall
On sky and ocean's bridal-hall.

The yellow river, broad and fleet,
Winds through its velvet meadows sweet—
A chain of gold for jewels meet.

Pours over all the sun's broad ray;
Power, beauty, peace, in one array!
My God, I thank Thee for this day.

# THE WIND

*Emily Dickinson*

Of all the sounds despatched abroad,
There's not a charge to me
Like that old measure in the boughs,
That phraseless melody

The wind does, working like a hand
Whose fingers brush the sky,
Then quiver down, with tufts of tune
Permitted gods and me.

When winds go round and round in bands,
And thrum upon the door,
And birds take places overhead,
To bear them orchestra,

I crave him grace, of summer boughs,
If such an outcast be,
He never heard that fleshless chant
Rise solemn in the tree,

As if some caravan of sound

On deserts, in the sky,

Had broken rank,

Then knit, and passed

In seamless company.

# THE RIVER

*Sara Teasdale*

I came from the sunny valleys
    And sought for the open sea,
For I thought in its gray expanses
    My peace would come to me.

I came at last to the ocean
    And found it wild and black,
And I cried to the windless valleys,
    "Be kind and take me back!"

But the thirsty tide ran inland,
    And the salt waves drank of me,
And I who was fresh as the rainfall
    Am bitter as the sea.

# WATER

*Ralph Waldo Emerson*

The water understands
Civilization well;
It wets my foot, but prettily
It chills my life, but wittily,
It is not disconcerted,
It is not broken-hearted:
Well used, it decketh joy,
Adorneth, doubleth joy:
Ill used, it will destroy,
In perfect time and measure
With a face of golden pleasure
Elegantly destroy.

# WHO ROBBED THE WOODS?

*Emily Dickinson*

Who robbed the woods,
The trusting woods?
The unsuspecting trees
Brought out their burrs and mosses
His fantasy to please.
He scanned their trinkets, curious,
He grasped, he bore away.
What will the solemn hemlock,
What will the fir-tree say?

# TO A BUTTERFLY

*William Wordsworth*

I've watched you now a full half-hour,
Self-poised upon that yellow flower;
And, little Butterfly! indeed
I know not if you sleep or feed.
More motionless! and then
How motionless!—not frozen seas
What joy awaits you, when the breeze
Hath found you out among the trees,
And calls you forth again;
This plot of orchard-ground is ours;
My trees they are, my Sister's flowers;
Here rest your wings when they are weary;
Here lodge as in a sanctuary!
Come often to us, fear no wrong;
Sit near us on the bough!
We'll talk of sunshine and of song,
And summer days when we were young;
Sweet childish days, that were as long
As twenty days are now.

# I WANDERED LONELY AS A CLOUD

*William Wordsworth*

I wandered lonely as a cloud
That floats on high o'er vales and hills,
When all at once I saw a crowd,
A host, of golden daffodils;
Beside the lake, beneath the trees,
Fluttering and dancing in the breeze.

Continuous as the stars that shine
And twinkle on the milky way,
They stretched in never-ending line
Along the margin of a bay:
Ten thousand saw I at a glance,
Tossing their heads in sprightly dance.

The waves beside them danced; but they
Out-did the sparkling waves in glee:
A poet could not but be gay,

In such a jocund company:
I gazed—and gazed—but little thought
What wealth the show to me had brought:

For oft, when on my couch I lie
In vacant or in pensive mood,
They flash upon that inward eye
Which is the bliss of solitude;
And then my heart with pleasure fills,
And dances with the daffodils.

# THE CLOUD

*Percy Bysshe Shelley*

I bring fresh showers for the thirsting flowers,
From the seas and the streams;
I bear light shade for the leaves when laid
In their noon-day dreams.
From my wings are shaken the dews that waken
The sweet buds every one,
When rocked to rest on their mother's breast,
As she dances about the sun.
I wield the flail of the lashing hail,
And whiten the green plains under,
And then again I dissolve it in rain,
And laugh as I pass in thunder.

I sift the snow on the mountains below,
And their great pines groan aghast;
And all the night 'tis my pillow white,
While I sleep in the arms of the blast.

Sublime on the towers of my skyey bowers,

Lightning my pilot sits,

In a cavern under is fettered the thunder,

It struggles and howls at fits;

Over earth and ocean, with gentle motion,

This pilot is guiding me,

Lured by the love of the genii that move

In the depths of the purple sea;

Over the rills, and the crags, and the hills,

Over the lakes and the plains,

Wherever he dream, under mountain or stream,

The Spirit he loves remains;

And I all the while bask in heaven's blue smile,

Whilst he is dissolving in rains.


The sanguine sunrise, with his meteor eyes,

And his burning plumes outspread,

Leaps on the back of my sailing rack,

When the morning star shines dead;

As on the jag of a mountain crag,

Which an earthquake rocks and swings,

An eagle alit one moment may sit

In the light of its golden wings.

And when sunset may breathe, from the lit sea beneath,

Its ardors of rest and of love,

And the crimson pall of eve may fall

From the depth of heaven above,

With wings folded I rest, on mine airy nest,

As still as a brooding dove.

That orbed maiden, with white fire laden,

Whom mortals call the moon,

Glides glimmering o'er my fleece-like floor,

By the midnight breezes strewn;

And wherever the beat of her unseen feet,

Which only the angels hear,

May have broken the woof of my tent's thin roof,

The stars peep behind her and peer;

And I laugh to see them whirl and flee,

Like a swarm of golden bees,

When I widen the rent in my windbuilt tent,

Till the calm rivers, lakes, and seas,

Like strips of the sky fallen thro' me on high,

Are each paved with the moon and these.


I bind the sun's throne with a burning zone,

And the moon's with a girdle of pearl;

The volcanoes are dim, and the stars reel and swim,

When the whirlwinds my banner unfurl.

From cape to cape, with a bridge-like shape,

Over a torrent sea,

Sunbeam-proof, I hang like a roof,

The mountains its columns be.

The triumphal arch thro' which I march,

With hurricane, fire, and snow,

When the powers of the air are chained to my chair,

Is the million-colored bow;

The sphere-fire above its soft colors wove,

Whilst the moist earth was laughing below.


I am the daughter of earth and water,

And the nursling of the sky;

I pass thro' the pores of the ocean and shores;

I change, but I cannot die.

For after the rain, when, with never a stain

The pavilion of heaven is bare,

And the winds and sunbeams with their convex gleams

Build up the blue dome of air,

I silently laugh at my own cenotaph,

And out of the caverns of rain,

Like a child from the womb, like a ghost from the tomb,

I arise and unbuild it again,

# THUNDER

*Joanna Baillie*

Spirit of strength, to whom in wrath 'tis given
To mar the earth, and shake the vasty heaven:
Behold the gloomy robes, that spreading hide
Thy secret majesty, lo! slow and wide,
Thy heavy skirts sail in the middle air,
Thy sultry shroud is o'er the noonday glare:
Th' advancing clouds sublimely roll'd on high,
Deep in their pitchy volumes clothe the sky;
Like hosts of gath'ring foes array'd in death,
Dread hangs their gloom upon the earth beneath,
It is thy hour: the awful deep is still,
And laid to rest the wind of ev'ry hill.
Wild creatures of the forest homeward scour,
And in their dens with fear unwonted cow'r.
Pride in the lordly palace is forgot,
And in the lowly shelter of the cot
The poor man sits, with all his fam'ly round,
In awful expectation of thy sound.

Lone on his way the trav'ller stands aghast;
The fearful looks of man to heav'n are cast,
When, lo! thy lightning gleams on high,
As swiftly turns his startled eye;
And swiftly as thy shooting blaze
Each half performed motion stays,
Deep awe, all human strife and labour stills,
And thy dread voice alone, the earth and heaven fills.

Bright bursts the lightning from the cloud's dark womb,
As quickly swallow'd in the closing gloom.
The distant streamy flashes, spread askance
In paler sheetings, skirt the wide expanse.
Dread flaming from aloft, the cat'ract dire
Oft meets in middle space the nether fire.
Fierce, red, and ragged, shiv'ring in the air,
Athwart mid-darkness shoots the lengthen'd glare.
Wild glancing round, the feebler lightning plays;
The rifted centre pours the gen'ral blaze;
And from the warring clouds in fury driven,
Red writhing falls the keen embodied bolt of heaven.

From the dark bowels of the burthen'd cloud
Dread swells the rolling peal, full, deep'ning, loud.
Wide ratt'ling claps the heavens scatter'd o'er,

In gathered strength lift the tremendous roar;
With weaning force it rumbles over head,
Then, growling, wears away to silence dread.
Now waking from afar in doubled might,
Slow rolling onward to the middle height;
Like crash of mighty mountains downward hurl'd,
Like the upbreaking of a wrecking world,
In dreadful majesty, th' explosion grand
Bursts wide, and awful, o'er the trembling land.
The lofty mountains echo back the roar,
Deep from afar rebounds earth's rocky shore;
All else existing in the senses bound
Is lost in the immensity of sound.
Wide jarring sounds by turns in strength convene,
And deep, and terrible, the solemn pause between.

   Aloft upon the mountain's side
The kindled forest blazes wide.
Huge fragments of the rugged deep
Are tumbled to the lashing deep.
Firm rooted in the cloven rock,
Loud crashing falls the stubborn oak.
The lightning keen, in wasteful ire,
Fierce darting on the lofty spire,

Wide rends in twain the ir'n-knit stone,

And stately tow'rs are lowly thrown.

Wild flames o'erscour the wide campaign,

And plough askance the hissing main.

Nor strength of man may brave the storm,

Nor shelter skreen the shrinking form;

Nor castle wall its fury stay,

Nor masy gate may bar its way.

It visits those of low estate,

It shakes the dwellings of the great,

It looks athwart the secret tomb,

And glares upon the prison's gloom;

While dungeons deep, in unknown light,

Flash hidious on the wretches' fight,

And lowly groans the downward cell,

Where deadly silence wont to dwell.


Now upcast eyes to heav'n adore,

And knees that never bow'd before.

In stupid wonder flares the child;

The maiden turns her glances wild,

And lifts to hear the coming roar:

The aged shake their locks so hoar:

And stoutest hearts begin to fail,

And many a manly cheek is pale;
Till nearer closing peals astound,
And crashing ruin mingles round;
Then 'numbing fear awhile up-binds
The pausing action of their minds,
Till wak'd to dreadful sense, they lift their eyes,
And round the stricken corse, shrill shrieks of horror rise.

Now thinly spreads the falling hall
A motly winter o'er the vale,
The hailstones bounding as they fall
On hardy rock, or storm-beat' wall.
The loud beginning peal its fury checks,
Now full, now fainter, with irreg'lar breaks,
Then weak in force, unites the scatter'd found;
And rolls its lengthen'd grumblings to the distant bound.
A thick and muddy whiteness clothes the sky,
In paler flashes gleams the lightning by;
And thro' the rent cloud, silver'd with his ray,
The sun looks down on all this wild affray;
As high enthron'd above all mortal ken,
A greater Pow'r beholds the strife of men:
Yet o'er the distant hills the darkness scowls,
And deep, and long, the parting tempest growls.

# A SERVICE OF SONG

*Emily Dickinson*

Some keep the Sabbath going to church;
I keep it staying at home,
With a bobolink for a chorister,
And an orchard for a dome.

Some keep the Sabbath in surplice;
I just wear my wings,
And instead of tolling the bell for church,
Our little sexton sings.

God preaches, — a noted clergyman, —
And the sermon is never long;
So instead of getting to heaven at last,
I'm going all along!

# THE MOUNTAIN'S FAITH

*Samuel Hall Young*

At eventide, upon a dreary sea,
I watched a mountain rear its hoary head
To look with steady gaze in the near heaven.
The earth was cold and still. No sound was heard
But the dream-voices of the sleeping sea.
The mountain drew its gray cloud-mantle close,
Like Roman senator, erect and old,
Raising aloft an earnest brow and calm,
With upward look intent of steadfast faith.
The sky was dim; no glory-light shone forth
To crown the mountain's faith; which faltered not,
But, ever hopeful, waited patiently.

At morn I looked again. Expectance sat
Of immanent glory on the mountain's brow.
And, in a moment, lo! the glory came!
An angel's hand rolled back a crimson cloud.

Deep, rose-red light of wondrous tone and power—
A crown of matchless splendor—graced its head,
Majestic, kingly, pure as Heaven, yet warm
With earthward love. A motion, like a heart
With rich blood beating, seemed to sway and pulse,
With might of ecstasy, the granite peak.
A poem grand it was of Love Divine—
An anthem, sweet and strong, of praise to God—
A victory-peal from barren fields of death.
Its gaze was heavenward still, but earthward too—
For Love seeks not her own, and joy is full,
Only when freest given. The sun shone forth,
And now the mountain doffed its ruby crown
For one of diamonds. Still the light streamed down;
No longer chill and bleak, the morning glowed
With warmth and light, and clouds of fiery hue
Mantled the crystal glacier's chilly stream,
And all the landscape throbbed with sudden joy.

# NATURE

*Ralph Waldo Emerson*

The patient Pan,
    Drunken with nectar,
    Sleeps or feigns slumber,
    Drowsily humming
    Music to the march of time.
    This poor tooting, creaking cricket,
    Pan, half asleep, rolling over
    His great body in the grass,
    Tooting, creaking,
    Feigns to sleep, sleeping never;
    'T is his manner,
    Well he knows his own affair,
    Piling mountain chains of phlegm
    On the nervous brain of man,
    As he holds down central fires
    Under Alps and Andes cold;
    Haply else we could not live,
    Life would be too wild an ode.

Come search the wood for flowers,—
    Wild tea and wild pea,
    Grapevine and succory,
    Coreopsis
    And liatris,
    Flaunting in their bowers;
    Grass with green flag half-mast high,
    Succory to match the sky,
    Columbine with horn of honey,
    Scented fern and agrimony;
    Forest full of essences
    Fit for fairy presences,
    Peppermint and sassafras,
    Sweet fern, mint and vernal grass,
    Panax, black birch, sugar maple,
    Sweet and scent for Dian's table,
    Elder-blow, sarsaparilla,
    Wild rose, lily, dry vanilla,—
    Spices in the plants that run
    To bring their first fruits to the sun.
    Earliest heats that follow frore
    Nervèd leaf of hellebore,
    Sweet willow, checkerberry red,

With its savory leaf for bread.

Silver birch and black
With the selfsame spice
Found in polygala root and rind,
Sassafras, fern, benzöine,
Mouse-ear, cowslip, wintergreen,
Which by aroma may compel
The frost to spare, what scents so well.

Where the fungus broad and red
Lifts its head,
Like poisoned loaf of elfin bread,
Where the aster grew
With the social goldenrod,
In a chapel, which the dew
Made beautiful for God:—
O what would Nature say?
She spared no speech to-day:
The fungus and the bulrush spoke,
Answered the pine-tree and the oak,
The wizard South blew down the glen,
Filled the straits and filled the wide,
Each maple leaf turned up its silver side.
All things shine in his smoky ray,

And all we see are pictures high;
Many a high hillside,
While oaks of pride
Climb to their tops,
And boys run out upon their leafy ropes.
The maple street
In the houseless wood,
Voices followed after,
Every shrub and grape leaf
Rang with fairy laughter.
I have heard them fall
Like the strain of all
King Oberon's minstrelsy.
Would hear the everlasting
And know the only strong?
You must worship fasting,
You must listen long.
Words of the air
Which birds of the air
Carry aloft, below, around,
To the isles of the deep,
To the snow-capped steep,
To the thundercloud.

For Nature, true and like in every place,
    Will hint her secret in a garden patch,
    Or in lone corners of a doleful heath,
    As in the Andes watched by fleets at sea,
    Or the sky-piercing horns of Himmaleh;
    And, when I would recall the scenes I dreamed
    On Adirondac steeps, I know
    Small need have I of Turner or Daguerre,
    Assured to find the token once again
    In silver lakes that unexhausted gleam
    And peaceful woods beside my cottage door.

What all the books of ages paint, I have.
    What prayers and dreams of youthful genius feign,
    I daily dwell in, and am not so blind
    But I can see the elastic tent of day
    Belike has wider hospitality
    Than my few needs exhaust, and bids me read
    The quaint devices on its mornings gay.
    Yet Nature will not be in full possessed,
    And they who truliest love her, heralds are
    And harbingers of a majestic race,
    Who, having more absorbed, more largely yield,
    And walk on earth as the sun walks in the sphere.

But never yet the man was found
　　Who could the mystery expound,
　　Though Adam, born when oaks were young,
　　Endured, the Bible says, as long;
　　But when at last the patriarch died
　　The Gordian noose was still untied.
　　He left, though goodly centuries old,
　　Meek Nature's secret still untold.

Atom from atom yawns as far
　　As moon from earth, or star from star.

When all their blooms the meadows flaunt
　　To deck the morning of the year,
　　Why tinge thy lustres jubilant
　　With forecast or with fear?

　　Teach me your mood, O patient stars!
　　Who climb each night the ancient sky,
　　Leaving on space no shade, no scars,
　　No trace of age, no fear to die.

The sun athwart the cloud thought it no sin
　　To use my land to put his rainbows in.

For joy and beauty planted it,
    With faerie gardens cheered,
    And boding Fancy haunted it
    With men and women weird.

What central flowing forces, say,
    Make up thy splendor, matchless day?

Day by day for her darlings to her much she added more;
    In her hundred-gated Thebes every chamber was a door,
    A door to something grander,—loftier walls, and vaster floor.

She paints with white and red the moors
    To draw the nations out of doors.

    A score of airy miles will smooth
    Rough Monadnoc to a gem.

# SUNSET IN THE GOLDEN GATE

*William E. Hutchinson*

When day is done there falls a solemn hush:
The birds are silent in their humble nest.
Then comes the Master Artist with his brush,
And paints with brilliant touch the golden west.

The blended colors sweep across the sky,
And add a halo at the close of day.
Their roseate hues far-reaching banners fly,
And gild the restless waters of the bay.

Mount Tamalpais stands in purple 'tire
Against the background, Phoenixlike, ornate:
Apollo drives his chariot of fire
Between the portals of the Golden Gate.

No other hand than His who rules on high,
Could wield the brush and spread such bright array
Upon the outstretched canvas of the sky,
Then draw the curtain of departing day.

# THE INWARD MORNING

*Henry David Thoreau*

Packed in my mind lie all the clothes
    Which outward nature wears,
And in its fashion's hourly change
    It all things else repairs.

In vain I look for change abroad,
    And can no difference find,
Till some new ray of peace uncalled
    Illumes my inmost mind.

What is it gilds the trees and clouds,
    And paints the heavens so gay,
But yonder fast-abiding light
    With its unchanging ray?

Lo, when the sun streams through the wood,
    Upon a winter's morn,
Where'er his silent beams intrude
    The murky night is gone.

How could the patient pine have known
        The morning breeze would come,
Or humble flowers anticipate
        The insect's noonday hum,—

Till the new light with morning cheer
        From far streamed through the aisles,
And nimbly told the forest trees
        For many stretching miles?

I've heard within my inmost soul
        Such cheerful morning news,
In the horizon of my mind
        Have seen such orient hues,

As in the twilight of the dawn,
        When the first birds awake,
Are heard within some silent wood,
        Where they the small twigs break,

Or in the eastern skies are seen,
        Before the sun appears,
The harbingers of summer heats
        Which from afar he bears.

# THE WHISPER OF THE EARTH

*Edward J. O'Brien*

In the misty hollow, shyly greening branches
Soften to the south wind, bending to the rain.
From the moistened earthland flutter little whispers,
Breathing hidden beauty, innocent of stain.
Little plucking fingers tremble through the grasses,
Little silent voices sigh the dawn of spring,
Little burning earth-flames break the awful stillness,
Little crying wind-sounds come before the King.
Powers, dominations urge the budding of the crocus,
Cherubim are singing in the moist cool stone,
Seraphim are calling through the channels of the lily,
God has heard the earth-cry and journeys to His throne.

# TREES

*Joyce Kilmer*

I think that I shall never see
A poem lovely as a tree.

A tree whose hungry mouth is prest
Against the earth's sweet flowing breast;

A tree that looks at God all day,
And lifts her leafy arms to pray;

A tree that may in Summer wear
A nest of robins in her hair;

Upon whose bosom snow has lain;
Who intimately lives with rain.

Poems are made by fools like me,
But only God can make a tree.

# EARTH

*John Hall Wheelock*

Grasshopper, your fairy song
And my poem alike belong
To the deep and silent earth
From which all poetry has birth;
All we say and all we sing
Is but as the murmuring
Of that drowsy heart of hers
When from her deep dream she stirs:
If we sorrow, or rejoice,
You and I are but her voice.

Deftly does the dust express
In mind her hidden loveliness,
And from her cool silence stream
The cricket's cry and Dante's dream:
For the earth that breeds the trees
Breeds cities too, and symphonies,
Equally her beauty flows
Into a savior or a rose.

Even as the growing grass
Up from the soil religions pass,
And the field that bears the rye
Bears parables and prophecy.
Out of the earth the poem grows
Like the lily, or the rose;
And all that man is or yet may be,
Is but herself in agony
Toiling up the steep ascent
Towards the complete accomplishment
When all dust shall be, the whole
Universe, one conscious soul.

Yea, and this my poem, too,
Is part of her as dust and dew,
Wherein herself she doth declare
Through my lips, and say her prayer.

# SUNRISE

*Ralph Waldo Emerson*

Would you know what joy is hid
In our green Musketaquid,
And for travelled eyes what charms
Draw us to these meadow farms,
Come and I will show you all
Makes each day a festival.
Stand upon this pasture hill,
Face the eastern star until
The slow eye of heaven shall show
The world above, the world below.

Behold the miracle!
Thou saw'st but now the twilight sad
And stood beneath the firmament,
A watchman in a dark gray tent,
Waiting till God create the earth,—
Behold the new majestic birth!
The mottled clouds, like scraps of wool,

Steeped in the light are beautiful.

What majestic stillness broods

Over these colored solitudes.

Sleeps the vast East in pleasèd peace,

Up the far mountain walls the streams increase

Inundating the heaven

With spouting streams and waves of light

Which round the floating isles unite:—

See the world below

Baptized with the pure element,

A clear and glorious firmament

Touched with life by every beam.

I share the good with every flower,

I drink the nectar of the hour:—

This is not the ancient earth

Whereof old chronicles relate

The tragic tales of crime and fate;

But rather, like its beads of dew

And dew-bent violets, fresh and new,

An exhalation of the time.

# THE FALL OF THE LEAF

*Henry David Thoreau*

Thank God who seasons thus the year,
   And sometimes kindly slants his rays;
For in his winter he's most near
   And plainest seen upon the shortest days.

Who gently tempers now his heats.
   And then his harsher cold, lest we
Should surfeit on the summer's sweets,
   Or pine upon the winter's crudity.

A sober mind will walk alone,
   Apart from nature, if need be,
And only its own seasons own:
   For nature leaving its humanity.

Sometimes a late autumnal thought
   Has crossed my mind in green July,

And to its early freshness brought
    Late ripened fruits, and an autumnal sky.

The evening of the year draws on,
    The fields a later aspect wear;
Since Summer's garishness is gone,
    Some grains of night tincture the noontide air.

Behold! the shadows of the trees
    Now circle wider 'bout their stem,
Like sentries that by slow degrees
    Perform their rounds, gently protecting them.

And as the year doth decline,
    The sun allows a scantier light;
Behind each needle of the pine
    There lurks a small auxiliar to the night.

I hear the cricket's slumbrous lay
    Around, beneath me, and on high;
It rocks the night, it soothes the day,
    And everywhere is Nature's lullaby.

But most he chirps beneath the sod,
    When he has made his winter bed;

His creak grown fainter but more broad,
A film of autumn o'er the summer spread.

Small birds, in fleets migrating by,
Now beat across some meadow's bay,
And as they tack and veer on high,
With faint and hurried click beguile the way.

Far in the woods, these golden days,
Some leaf obeys its Maker's call;
And through their hollow aisles it plays
With delicate touch the prelude of the Fall.

Gently withdrawing from its stem,
It lightly lays itself along
Where the same hand hath pillowed them,
Resigned to sleep upon the old year's throng.

The loneliest birch is brown and sere,
The farthest pool is strewn with leaves,
Which float upon their watery bier,
Where is no eye that sees, no heart that grieves.

The jay screams through the chestnut wood;
The crisped and yellow leaves around

Are hue and texture of my mood,
    And these rough burs my heirlooms on the ground.


The threadbare trees, so poor and thin,
    They are no wealthier than I;
But with as brave a core within
    They rear their boughs to the October sky.


Poor knights they are which bravely wait
    The charge of Winter's cavalry,
Keeping a simple Roman state,
    Discumbered of their Persian luxury.

# REFLECTIONS

*Alfred Castner King*

On the margin of a lakelet,
　　In a rugged mountain clime,
Where precipice and pinnacle
　　Of countenance sublime,
Cast their weird, austere reflections
　　In the water's glistening sheen,
I strolled in contemplative mood,
　　Both pensive and serene.

As in a crystal mirror,
　　In that lakelet's placid face,
I saw the mountains upside down,
　　With all their pristine grace;
I saw each cliff and point of rocks,
　　I saw the stately pine,
Inverted in fantastic form
　　Below the water line.

I paused in admiration;
     And with calm complacency
I marveled at this photograph
     From nature's gallery;
And as my eyes surveyed the scene
     With solemn grandeur fraught,
This simile flashed through my mind
     As instantly as thought:

As the stern, majestic mountains,
     Without error or mistake,
Were reflected in the bosom
     Of that cool, pellucid lake,
So our every thought and action,
     Be it deed of hate or love,
May be photographed in record
     In that gallery above.

# THE MOSQUITO

*D. H. Lawrence*

When did you start your tricks
Monsieur?

What do you stand on such high legs for?
Why this length of shredded shank
You exaltation?

Is it so that you shall lift your centre of gravity upwards
And weigh no more than air as you alight upon me,
Stand upon me weightless, you phantom?

I heard a woman call you the Winged Victory
In sluggish Venice.
You turn your head towards your tail, and smile.

How can you put so much devilry
Into that translucent phantom shred
Of a frail corpus?

Queer, with your thin wings and your streaming legs
How you sail like a heron, or a dull clot of air,
A nothingness.

Yet what an aura surrounds you;
Your evil little aura, prowling, and casting a numbness
    on my mind.

That is your trick, your bit of filthy magic:
Invisibility, and the anæsthetic power
To deaden my attention in your direction.

But I know your game now, streaky sorcerer.

Queer, how you stalk and prowl the air
In circles and evasions, enveloping me,
Ghoul on wings
Winged Victory.

Settle, and stand on long thin shanks
Eyeing me sideways, and cunningly conscious that I
    am aware,
You speck.

I hate the way you lurch off sideways into air
Having read my thoughts against you.

Come then, let us play at unawares,
And see who wins in this sly game of bluff.
Man or mosquito.

You don't know that I exist, and I don't know that
   you exist.
Now then!

It is your trump
It is your hateful little trump
You pointed fiend,
Which shakes my sudden blood to hatred of you:
It is your small, high, hateful bugle in my ear.

Why do you do it?
Surely it is bad policy.

They say you can't help it.

If that is so, then I believe a little in Providence
   protecting the innocent.
But it sounds so amazingly like a slogan
A yell of triumph as you snatch my scalp.

Blood, red blood
Super-magical
Forbidden liquor.

I behold you stand
For a second enspasmed in oblivion,
Obscenely ecstasied
Sucking live blood
My blood.

Such silence, such suspended transport,
Such gorging,
Such obscenity of trespass.

You stagger
As well as you may.
Only your accursed hairy frailty
Your own imponderable weightlessness
Saves you, wafts you away on the very draught my
    anger makes in its snatching.

Away with a pæan of derision
You winged blood-drop.

Can I not overtake you?
Are you one too many for me
Winged Victory?
Am I not mosquito enough to out-mosquito you?

Queer, what a big stain my sucked blood makes
Beside the infinitesimal faint smear of you!
Queer, what a dim dark smudge you have
    disappeared into!

# BIRCHES

*Robert Frost*

When I see birches bend to left and right
Across the lines of straighter darker trees,
I like to think some boy's been swinging them.
But swinging doesn't bend them down to stay.
Ice-storms do that. Often you must have seen them
Loaded with ice a sunny winter morning
After a rain. They click upon themselves
As the breeze rises, and turn many-coloured
As the stir cracks and crazes their enamel.
Soon the sun's warmth makes them shed crystal
      shells
Shattering and avalanching on the snow-crust—
Such heaps of broken glass to sweep away
You'd think the inner dome of heaven had fallen.
They are dragged to the withered bracken by the
      load,
And they seem not to break; though once they are
      bowed

So low for long, they never right themselves:
You may see their trunks arching in the woods
Years afterwards, trailing their leaves on the ground,
Like girls on hands and knees that throw their hair
Before them over their heads to dry in the sun.
But I was going to say when Truth broke in
With all her matter-of-fact about the ice-storm,
I should prefer to have some boy bend them
As he went out and in to fetch the cows—
Some boy too far from town to learn baseball,
Whose only play was what he found himself,
Summer or winter, and could play alone.
One by one he subdued his father's trees
By riding them down over and over again
Until he took the stiffness out of them,
And not one but hung limp, not one was left
For him to conquer. He learned all there was
To learn about not launching out too soon
And so not carrying the tree away
Clear to the ground. He always kept his poise
To the top branches, climbing carefully
With the same pains you use to fill a cup
Up to the brim, and even above the brim.

Then he flung outward, feet first, with a swish,
Kicking his way down through the air to the ground.
So was I once myself a swinger of birches.
And so I dream of going back to be.
It's when I'm weary of considerations,
And life is too much like a pathless wood
Where your face burns and tickles with the cobwebs
Broken across it, and one eye is weeping
From a twig's having lashed across it open.
I'd like to get away from earth awhile
And then come back to it and begin over.
May no fate wilfully misunderstand me
And half grant what I wish and snatch me away
Not to return. Earth's the right place for love:
I don't know where it's likely to go better.
I'd like to go by climbing a birch tree,
And climb black branches up a snow-white trunk
Toward heaven, till the tree could bear no more,
But dipped its top and set me down again.
That would be good both going and coming back.
One could do worse than be a swinger of birches.

## ABOUT BUSHEL & PECK BOOKS

Bushel & Peck Books is a children's publishing house with a special mission. Through our Book-for-Book Promise™, we donate one book to kids in need for every book we sell. Our beautiful books are given to kids through schools, libraries, local neighborhoods, shelters, nonprofits, and also to many selfless organizations that are working hard to make a difference. So thank you for purchasing this book! Because of you, another book will make its way into the hands of a child who needs it most.

## NOMINATE A SCHOOL OR ORGANIZATION TO RECEIVE FREE BOOKS

Do you know a school, library, or organization that could use some free books for their kids? We'd love to help! Please fill out the nomination form on our website (see below), and we'll do everything we can to make something happen.

www.bushelandpeckbooks.com/pages/
nominate-a-school-or-organization

If you liked this book, please leave a review online at your favorite retailer. Honest reviews spread the word about Bushel & Peck—and help us make better books, too!